# I Am
# a Poet,
# but I Didn't
# Know It!

J E S S I E   R I S E R

PAGE PUBLISHING, INC.
New York, NY

First originally published by Page Publishing, Inc. 2019

ISBN 978-1-64544-490-9 (Paperback)
ISBN 978-1-64544-491-6 (Digital)

Printed in the United States of America

Oklahoma City Tragedy
It was not pretty.
This should not happen to no other city.
The United States president has made it so clear
that the American people will not live in fear.
Those that are responsible for this deed,
that is the end of their lives, and they won't ever succeed.
If you live in the United States
and you want to do wrong,
find another country and make that your home.
Our hearts go out to every woman, child, and man.
And to all of the rescue workers
of the American Heartland.
Let's count our blessing.
This is not the end of the story.
We as American people are still proud of Old Glory.

Walking along one of my favorite spots;
I'm looking for money,
but I'm pretending I'm not;
my head is going up and down
every other step
my eyes are focusing from the right to the left,
but the odds are against me,
that I won't make a find;
I'm so broke,
I'll pick up a dime.
Isn't it strange that we all have been this way?
Some of us will admit it,
but some of us will not say;
when we do have money that eliminates the frown;
our heads are up high,
and we have no reason to look down.

I can't go home anymore.
There is no house to be seen.
My mother and father are gone now.
But they are still in my dreams.
All the places that I use to play
are now covered with trees.
I go and visit it sometimes,
but for hours I don't want to leave.
Trying to hold my head up to walk away and be proud
as I made two steps,
I found myself crying out loud.
Now the torch has been passed.
Let's run long,
let's run hard.
As long as we are running for Jesus,
I'll get a chance to see my God.

Getting relaxed so I can watch the game.
I don't want anyone to call my name.
The stage is set for an exciting time.
This is my day to unwind.
I've got everything I need except my cup,
but I'm so comfortable I hate to get up.
Looking at the clock it's hard to ignore.
Then I heard a knock,
Oh, it's someone at the door.
The game came on just as I arose.
I said to myself, *I should have locked both doors.*
Finally opened it and looked into two eyes,
and what I saw, boy was I surprised.
An officer said, "This is not your day,
we have two parking tickets that you forgot to pay."

My love for you is real.
And I will always be true.
All my friends tell me
that I shouldn't be weak for you.
When Cupid shot his arrow,
they don't know it went all the way through.
But I am one of many, and you are one of few
that knows when a person is madly in love with you.
My hope is only one day
that you can see it through.
When we walk down the aisle,
we both can say I do.

To speak of love is only a word.
If it's to the right person, you may be heard.
When you have two that are so endowed,
if it's not for real, they will soon find out.
To fall in love is a great feeling.
Stay true to whom you are dealing.
Listen to the bees.
Then listen to the birds.
Your purpose in life may have been served.

Children are precious
when they are very small.
The gift of life overwhelms us all.
Growing up so young
we wanted to have so many.
Some of us are grown now,
and we don't have any.
Going to bed at night
sometimes makes us feel bad
that we don't hear little voices saying,
"Good night, Mom and Dad."

While I'm sitting here under the trees,
listening to the birds and enjoying the breeze.
As I began to look around,
then I heard a familiar sound.
Slowly turning so I could see,
there was a big buck looking straight at me.
He frightened me so bad,
I let out a yell
and then all I could see was his pretty white tail.
When you are out in the woods
and you hear a sound,
don't forget to always look around.

Lying on the beach,
trying to get a tan;
my head is elevated,
and my feet is in the sand.
It is a nice day.
The sun is shining bright.
I am so relaxed.
I could stay here all night.
The sun is going down.
There are no more rays.
My tan is looking great.
I'm looking forward to better days.

Fishing in the morning gives me a chill.
But arriving early gives me a thrill.
Finally got that spot you had seen days before.
When everybody was catching them
and pulling them out by the score.
When they are biting, it is a lot of fun.
If you can brave the mosquitoes and the blazing sun.
The day has come to an end.
As I began to frown,
I'm thinking about that long ways
I have to drive back to town.
When I get home upon my throne, I'll sat
and smile when they say, "Did you catch that?"

Working hard every day is no big deal.
But I don't make enough money to pay my bills.
I ask my boss to give me a raise,
but he suggested I work more days.
I'm up to seven now and that's not enough.
My wife is expecting and it's getting pretty rough.
As time went on, we had a little boy.
To my wife and I, he's a bundle of joy.
Taking care of him I'll do my part.
Going in every day, I don't mind working hard.

Computerized systems are the new thing.
We can punch a few buttons,
without using our brains.
It makes it easier,
but how long will it last?
If we keep it cybernetic,
it will be a thing of the past.
To all of you, computer whizzes,
just be cool,
and think about all of the high school students
that are coming out of school.
Let them have an opportunity to cash in,
who knows,
one day they may be your friend.

Up and down as the world goes;
And we are in the seams;
some of us are fortunate
that we can live out our dreams.
The rest of us are still blessed
to even be alive,
especially in the United States
and not on the other side.

Traveling by air you can climb so high.
It's a beautiful sunset
from the clouds in the sky.
Although I am hoping to get there on time,
when the plane lands that will ease my mind.
I ask the cabdriver if he would let me use a phone
to call my girlfriend to see if she was still at home.
When no one answered, I continued to her house.
I love her a lot, and I want her to be my spouse.
Knocked on the door and she finally let me in.
There sitting on her bed,
she introduced me as her friend.
With tears in my eyes,
I slowly walked toward the door.
She whispered to me softly,
"I don't love you anymore."

All the way through high school
I tried hard to achieve.
But when I entered my senior year,
I did not want to leave.
The thought of leaving my friends all at the same time,
some of them I'll never see again,
and that really blew my mind.
Now I have entered the outside world,
and it is kind of strange.
The pressure is on me to do good,
and uphold my family name.
Thirty-five years has passed,
and all my kids are grown.
My wife and I are happy now.
We have just bought a brand-new home.
So to all of the high school students,
don't think negative and be a fool.
The world has everything to offer you.
But the trick is to stay in school.

Sitting at this desk with my head in my hand;
thinking I'm glad God made me a man.
A man is a man, but he's a man alone.
If he don't have a woman,
someone to call his own.
When love strikes them and they start to click,
the bond is tighter than a mason's brick.
After the wedding is over they start to enjoy,
the pleasure of having, a girl or a boy.

It is cold outside,
and the buses are running slow.
I will be careful who I tell again,
that I don't love them anymore.
It is icy cold out here,
and I can barely see the ground.
I have to make my steps carefully
because I'm worried about slipping down.
When I do get on the bus, I hope the heater is on,
so my blood can start back circulating
and my body will feel nice and warm.
I saw something, I did not want to see,
so I made a stand.
I had to tell her face-to-face
that I could no longer be her man.
Now my heart is broken,
but it's something that had to be done.
Telling your lover you don't love them anymore,
is never a lot of fun.

Why does why
sometimes mean goodbye?
I was standing tall,
with my back to the wall,
sometimes it is better to know,
before you walk through the door.
I took a big chance,
when I started to dance.
She said, "I am alone,
you might take me home."
Then he stood up,
and knocked over my cup.
He looked into my eyes,
and I apologized.
Then I started to see
that she was not for me.
But I will never say why,
just only goodbye.

I need a vacation,
and I need it fast.
I don't know how long,
my mentality is going to last.
Been working hard,
seven days a week,
my old body has finally
reached its peak.

Went to bed late last night.
Studying for a test,
I am going to take my time,
and hope for the best.
If I do good
and have a passing score,
I'll be excused
and won't have to take it anymore.
I'll relax, smile, and grin,
and look across the room.
And wave to all of my friends.

The last job I had.
I wanted to change it so bad.
When I went home,
I was usually all alone,
my wife said, "Can't you see?
It's not enough money
for you and me."
As time went by,
things have changed.
Now my wife has a new name,
this goes to show
if you can't provide,
all you will be left with
is your pride.

It is a proven fact
that if you don't go to school,
when you get of age,
you will surely be a fool.
Education is important
when you're trying to get ahead.
If you don't have a job,
all you can do is lie in bed.
God has blessed America
to be the United States.
You can always go back to school,
it is never too late.

Unauthorized people should not drive,
if they want to stay alive.
When you drive, stay alert.
Follow the rules,
and you won't be hurt.
If your car spins out of control,
but you know you have been told.
So if you drive, don't drive fast.
The slower you drive,
the longer you'll last.
Better yet, don't even drive,
get your license first
and you will be authorized.

Understanding is the best thing in the world.
And we do understand
that a boy is different from a girl.
If you understand what is required of you,
the world will open up,
and you can go straight through.
A good understanding is what we all need
that would keep us smiling,
and we wouldn't have to grieve.
A bad understanding,
"Oh no," that's not for me.
But I'll never let it get in the way
of supporting my family tree.

Driving home from work today,
I didn't expect the big delay.
Looking at cars from all around,
but I was still downtown.
As I turned the radio on
and listening to my favorite song,
then I looked up and began to see,
there was a big truck headed straight for me.
As I turned and started to yield
then I realized he had lost his wheel.
Being the driver that I am,
I sped up, and I started to scram.
So when you are in traffic,
don't start to groan
because big trucks are also headed home.

Perhaps you know,
just how I feel.
When I stuffed myself
and had a good meal.
Holidays are great,
around this time.
Everybody is fit
and doing just fine.
Introduced the newborns
to the family clan
and when we pray together,
let us all hold hands.

Today, I didn't get my check on time.
My rent is due, and I haven't got a dime.
My wife is pouting and she's real mad.
The kids are upset and they look pretty sad.
I got down on my knees,
and I started to pray.
I said, "Lord, please help me make it through the day."
The telephone rang,
he said his name was Mel.
He wanted to know was my car still for sale.
Now we are the happiest family in our neighborhood.
So when you are having a problem,
and it is too much for you,
Call on the Lord, he knows just what to do.

Sometimes you'll dream,
and you don't want it to come true.
Somebody is in that dream
and they are not being nice to you.
Another time you'll dream
and you'll wake up with a yell.
Then you'll take a deep breath
because you thought you were going to hell.
If we could control our dreams,
now that would be great.
We all would be at work on time,
and we'll have no reason to be late.

Whenever a child starts to cry,
a good mother is always nearby.
I can't remember my first tear,
but her name has always been Mother Dear.
Growing up from yesterday,
I can now truly say,
"If every mother would be so sweet,
being alive could be a treat."
Thinking back to the things I thought I knew,
I see now that they were so few.
She always showed me the way,
so I could see another day.
And to you it should be no doubt,
That…is who I am talking about.

God, please help us to be strong,
when our loved one leaves us,
and we are all alone.
I lie in bed at night wondering how can this be.
I never thought that she would ever leave me.
I don't know where she went,
but I'm looking here and there.
I miss that smiling face and that pretty long hair.
Don't for one second think that this can't be true.
It just happened to me,
and it can also happen to you.

Looking out of the window of the greyhound bus,
I didn't know American farmers
could raise so much stuff.
There is a little crop here
and a big crop there,
an abundance of greenery that is growing everywhere.
As I travel along these beautiful sites,
I would like for days to be long
and very short nights.
So hail to the farmers,
keep us eating good,
and we'll stay healthy like we know we should.

I love you so much;
it hurts me to breathe;
my heart would break if you decided to leave.
If love was food,
I would weigh two thousand pounds;
Just love me back,
and I will always stay fat and round.

Went out last night with nothing on my mind,
as twelve o'clock rolled around,
I was having a good time dancing all around
until the break of dawn.
Looked down at my feet,
I didn't have any shoes on.
Got home somehow and finally went to bed,
all through the night,
I was grabbing my aching head.
When the sun came up and to my surprise,
there was a person next to me looking into my eyes.
I turned and said to her, "What are you doing here?"
Then she said to me without having any fear,
"You should never ever drink another beer."

We need to pray a prayer
for these that are living.
And those that went before us,
we thank God for giving.
We know by faith just who we are
and where we would like to be
when we see that morning star.
When you'll reach a certain age,
you know you have been told
that God is for real,
deep down in your soul.

What I know about a man,
I can simply write a book.
A man is not a man
because of the way he look.
Getting respect from another man,
it is something he will have to earn.
Giving respect in order to receive it,
it is something he will have to learn.
Younger men and older men,
let's all make a vow
and take care of our responsibilities
when we do make a child.
If you do what is required of you,
a woman will shake your hand.
I know that for a fact
because I am also a man.

Opportunity for success is always great.
But it is only prevalent in the United States.
Strive for your goals,
but you have to apply.
Take the honest approach
and try not to lie.
If you lie once, you'll have to lie again.
When you get caught,
you won't have any more friends.

I entered the armed services,
while you were still around.
My mother informed me later
that you had left town.
I am so in love with you,
something that you didn't know.
When I go to bed at night,
I wondered where did you go.
Five years has gone by now,
and my love is still strong.
Somebody find her please
and ask her to come back home.
Sitting outside one day talking to my friend, Larry,
he said, "That lady you are in love with
has recently gotten married."
I fell to my knees with tears in my eyes.
I ask God why me as I looked to the skies.
I wish you all the happiness in everything you do.
My mistake is not telling you how much I love you.

The "lovebug" has bitten me,
and it hit me hard.
I got caught slipping,
and didn't put up my guard.
Now I am hers and she is all mine,
and we should be together until the end of time.
So thanks to the "lovebug" don't ever bite me again;
not only is she my wife,
she's also my best friend.

I want to talk about a city without calling a name.
If your city is guilty then you can share the blame.
I drive in your city almost every day.
Tell me why your comrades refuses to sway.
They will pull out in front of you
without making a sound.
Either you drive their speed
or you can go around.
If the shoe was on the other foot
and they pulled out real slow,
that made you late for work.
Then you'll reap just what you sow.

Looking back in time,
when I didn't have a dime.
Follow your dreams, and don't give up.
You may not drink from the bitter cup.
I was told that one day,
now I am proud to say,
"You know the future is on my mind,
and I will never look back in time."

With grace and charm,
she swept me off of my feet.
Seemed as though I was watching her from a mile,
but she was only across the street.
As strong as I thought I was,
my heart weakened and started to flutter.
As I approached her and started to speak,
my voice left me, and I started to stutter.
She had smooth skin and a beautiful face,
for her I would do anything.
I viewed her finger and was devastated,
after seeing a wedding ring.
Now it is all over,
and I can stop thinking about what might have been.
But I won't stop looking for that special someone,
if it takes me to the end.

CPSIA information can be obtained
at www.ICGtesting.com
Printed in the USA
LVHW111046231219
641444LV00004B/735/P